BEASTS IN
& SNOW

The following poems have been previously published in *In Praise of Pedagogy,* edited by Wendy Bishop and David Starkey (Calendar Island Press, 2000): "Teaching Reading," "Stone Dreams," and "Roses and Tulips."

"Blue Flags" first appeared in *Intermountain Woman.*

"You shouldn't do this" first appeared in *English Journal.*

The lines of the Psalms in the first section come from *The Book of Common Prayer* (Oxford University Press, 1969).

BEASTS IN
& SNOW

JANE ELKINGTON WOHL

HIGH PLAINS PRESS

POETRY OF THE AMERICAN WEST SERIES

Cover photograph © Diana Volk
Used with permission of the photographer

FIRST PRINTING

1 3 5 7 9 8 6 4 2

Library of Congress Cataloging-in-Publication Data

Wohl, Jane Elkington.
Beasts in snow / Jane Elkington Wohl.
p. cm. -- (Poetry of the American West)
ISBN 0-931271-78-9 (limited edition hardcover : alk. paper) --
ISBN 0-931271-79-7 (pbk. : alk. paper)
1. Teacher-student relationships--Poetry. 2. West (U.S.)--Poetry. 3.
Teaching--Poetry. 4. Nature--Poetry. I. Title. II. Series.
PS3623.O45B43 2005
811'.6--dc22

2005001921

HIGH PLAINS PRESS
539 CASSA ROAD
GLENDO, WY 82213
1-800-552-7819

CATALOGUE AVAILABLE
www.highplainspress.com

For Harriet F. Elkington and Norma S. Wohl
with love and admiration

CONTENTS

INTRICACIES OF GRACE

WHERE WE ARE NOW

INTRICACIES
& OF GRACE

PSALM 1

Blessed is the man that hath not walked in the
council of the ungodly, nor in the way of sinners:
and hath not sat in the seat of the scornful.

Dainis brings me fresh eggs
and we cross the street to look
into windows of the empty house
where my neighbor died this spring.

"No room for my goats in the yard,"
he tells me, Lily, Snow Poem,
Gretel, and one whose name
I always forget. He milks each day,
feels the soft skin, warm full udders.
Gifts of cheese arrive at odd times on
my kitchen counter. I can tell
there's some appeal to living in town,

but then it's their eyes,
those rectangular golden pupils
and the stillness, the wood smoke rising
above the craggy apple orchard,
nine pheasant chicks, deer in the trees
and soft apples falling. ✑

PSALM 2

Why do the heathen so furiously rage together: and why
do the people imagine a vain thing?

Wells River in winter
held behind still beaver ponds
maple branches against sky
bare willow stems

At the bend
remains of Ricker's mill
mill stones sunk deep into earth
frozen over, perhaps a cellar hole

Our road rises into second growth forest
above the open valley floor
tires like mill wheels on blacktop
snow skiffs in front of headlights
advances, retreats.
We move upstream. &

Psalm 5

Ponder my words, O Lord: consider my meditation.

Edward Taylor considered the lone wasp on
his winter window sill, watched it lift
thin legs to groom its head. His eyes upon
the insect, he gloried in God, did not feel left
out of the Holy World. The creature only
served to show him the intricacies of grace.
Today my fall flowers begin to open slowly.
Each one unfolds, reveals an inner face
of purple, orange, gold. Green leaves
surround these blooms, immune to early autumn
winds and rain. Taylor knew that summer grieves
itself to fall which in turn precedes winter's tomb
of cold and ice. And yet, thin legs, the finest wings
survive, and we listen while a flashing cardinal sings. ❧

PSALM 10

Why standest thou so far off, O Lord: and hidest thy
face in the needful time of trouble?

a muddy puddle
sparrows
my neighbor's empty house

a swarm of gnats
evening light
dancing

driving today
a red-tail hawk
a gray fence post

my neighbor's empty house
blind windows
grass still growing &

PSALM 13

How long wilt thou forget me, O Lord, for ever: how
long wilt thou hide thy face from me?

Worms have no eyes,
but feel light through their skins.

Singing today all sound is light,
Italian words like rain.

Immediate vibration stops; the air
continues.

We don't know what we have heard. &

BEASTS IN SNOW

PSALM 15

Lord, who shall dwell in thy tabernacle: or who shall rest
on the holy hill?

Mary Ann shows me the iris she has transplanted
into another friend's yard
in preparation for her own move
back to town.
"This one came west," she tells me,
"in a covered wagon. It's just deep purple,
nothing unusual."
Nothing, I think, but history.

We are together again for the first time
in twelve years,
and she tells me all the plants:
the little spruce tree she's planted
by the garage, "just until I find a place,
but it wanted to be out of its pot so bad,"
another iris, a hybrid, narrow leaves
and flowers of some undetermined color,
some pink thing, "it might not do well here,
this isn't really the right climate,"
another plant "you can't see it yet, but it's just a
ground cover."

INTRICACIES OF GRACE

And lavender, without even thinking she
breaks off a piece, crumples in it her fingers,
hands it to me to smell, as if we've done
this exchange before.

"Judy's afraid I'll come and dig all these up,
take them away when I finally move here,"
she says as the sun warms our shoulders, arms,
bare feet, "but she doesn't know how much
they spread." ❧

PSALM 16

Preserve me, O God: for in thee have I put my trust.

Jake tells me that .3333 repeating
plus .6666 repeating adds up to .9999 repeating
or really to one because one-third plus two-thirds is one,
while some of his classmates argue that
it's not the same, that somewhere out beyond
the farthest nine some undefined space exists.

I discuss the ambiguities of punctuation
with my English classes and watch my students
struggle with the idea that one plus one is not
always two, but has more to do with intent
than fact, that a misplaced comma can, but doesn't
always change a meaning.

A note played alone is meaningless.
Mozart depends on individual notes
only in combination.

Rachel stands at the piano,
her voice barely above a whisper.
She sings as if she is afraid we'll listen
until Gene tells her to direct the tone,
to send it through him. The music is pure
and sweet, not just one single note alone,
but Rachel's concentration, her voice,
her thought reaching out to him.

We are always reaching for that space,
the interstices between nerve and nerve,
the sound that crosses it, the way a breath
will leave our mouths and then condense white
in winter air, the way sometimes we hear the voice
of someone far away, remember half a face or
stretch to cross that tiny gap between .9999 and one. ❧

PSALM 19

The heavens declare the glory of God: and the firmament
sheweth his handywork.

Like worms with no eyes, we see light
through our skins, our hearts and lungs blossom,
turn, like great sunflowers, to the sun.
The balloon in my chest breaks against black branches,
tangles, struggles to escape on wind.

Birds flock like Morse code across
the February sky. Dots and dashes swooping
in some language eyes can't read. Tomorrow's
sun rises like Columbus on some unknown ocean.

Some days I wish I were like Galileo's daughter
in her convent sending letters, like small birds,
to her father. Reading what he sent winging back,
going into the garden at night to see the stars as he saw them,
not like jewels on velvet, but worlds spinning out past
knowing, feeling light coming in through her skin, too dark
for eyes, knowing how great an un-knowing, like hunger,
possessed him. &

Psalm 22

My God, my God, look upon me; why hast thou forsaken me: and
art so far from my health, and from the words of my complaint?

She hangs completely in the balance,
waiting for rescue. We watch her save
kittens mewing at her apartment door.

One day last summer, she cried as a beetle died,
its small carapace in her dirt-stained hand.
I wiped her face. "Part of the food chain,"
I told her smelling the smoke in her hair,
seeing the chipped polish on her nails.

She worries that the world she knows will collapse
and wants to wait it out on some Caribbean Island,
as the world she knows falls around her,
bills unpaid, schoolwork undone.

Only the cats get fed. &

BEASTS IN SNOW

PSALM 24

The earth is the Lord's and all that therein is: the compass of the
world, and they that dwell therein.

February Morning:

> Like smoke and mirrors
> mist rises from Little Goose Creek.
>
> The sky restrains impending snow.
>
> Frost rimes the willows' thin fingers
> reaching up along the bank.
>
> Phantoms in a ghost-scape,
> three gray deer slip across the far field,
> flick white tails, black-tipped ears.
> They move on the periphery,
> beyond the faint fenceline, gray posts and wire.
>
> Last night an owl called across the snowy draw. &

PSALM 27

The Lord is my light, and my salvation; whom then shall I fear: the
Lord is the strength of my life; of whom then shall I be afraid?

At the beginning of hunting season
the deer stop coming to the yard,
no longer walk the street in the early morning.
Their small black hooves don't click on the pavement,
don't make the sound of early rain.

The October sky pearls above the pastel draw,
colors neutral and vibrant as the deer, a fleck of white,
a flare of sumac, that sage-green, not quite grey,
the gold burnished almost to silver, almost to nothing.
The deer hide where grey becomes green
becomes silver becomes white becomes light.

We don't see their tall ears flick at the sound
of an opening door, or see them turn to look
at us with wide deep eyes as we stand,
still sleepy in our blowing nightgowns.

They hide somewhere in the tangles of the draw,
in the over-growth of willow scrub, hawthorn,
raspberry canes and grass turned gold. &

BEASTS IN SNOW

PSALM 42

*Like as the hart desireth the waterbrooks; so longeth my soul
after thee, O God.*

Three deer cross the street this morning,
pale flanks in the early sun.
Ears tense, they startle at a slamming door,
an engine's cough,
turn down the alley toward the shelter
of the draw.

Yesterday I read William Stafford to my students,
the poem about the dead deer on the road,
her still-warm belly, the red taillights
of the car. They waited, wanting
the happy ending, wanting him to do
the heroic and unreasonable act.

I glimpsed Rebecca putting on fresh lipstick
just before her class, an act as commonplace
as breath, her eyes wide, concentrated
on the mirror's light. I could almost see
the night's eyeshine reflecting back
at file cabinet, computer desk and papers.

Later, she sits with students in the hall
explaining words, phrases, clauses,
the unexplainable ways words connect and change,
the way a misplaced noun can shift a sentence
as subtly as mist, as evening light, the way a sound
becomes the click of hooves on morning streets.

We stand on narrow roads in darkness,
in the soft glow of crimson taillights, in billowing exhaust.
Our hands momentarily feel the life beneath the skin,
the way the warmth still rises through our fingers,
and finally, unwitnessed, we do what must be done. ❧

PSALM 49

*Hear ye this, all ye people: ponder it with your ears, all ye that dwell
in the world.*

It was only to check the size tag, the washing instructions
of the swirling rayon skirt: I pulled at the waistband and felt
the trough of skin where it curves in toward
the straight line of her spine.

Later, I read student poems,
Trent's, full of adolescent bright lights,
mirrors, pierced lips, tongues, eyebrows,
incense, fast cars, inarticulate longing.

The smoke-blue sweater rode just at her hips.
We went back to the music, to the controlled breathing of voice class,
and the repeated, practiced repertoire.
A string of tiny coral beads hung at her neck.

He writes of music stores, too much coffee
and compresses many trips to Billings into one
filled with all the things he'll never say,
the way once, at 15, I danced in the midnight fountains
of New York's Seagram building,
sandals dangling from tiny straps in my hands.

I remember, now, with this pile of poems,
her skin against my fingers, that brief edge
of intimacy, how in that room of singers,
there was, momentarily, something beyond sound. ❧

PSALM 50

The Lord, even the most mighty God, hath spoken: and called the world,
from the rising up of the sun unto the going down thereof.

In Hiroshige's print, "Moonlight – Nagakubo" the figures
crossing the bridge are weary. Their backs
slump forward, even the horse plods
behind the man who leads.
The rider seems to sleep, head bent under a bamboo hat.

Evening: he has hidden most of the full moon behind
a full-leafed tree.

The edges of the day intrigue us, the way
the wood block opened possibilities to the artist
awakening at dawn, seeing in his mind's eye
the moon, the bridge, the weary travelers.

He cut into grain, cutting away to reveal the bridge
where the paper's white becomes the full moon's light
on water. Eventually he will add color, the foreground, shadowed blue.

But the weary people on the bridge, the full moon
partially obscured by the central tree:
these are what concerned him, these figures at the end of day. ❧

BEASTS IN SNOW

Psalm 52

Why boastest thou thyself, thou tyrant: that thou canst do mischief?

> when a child is dying
> no motel room is safe
> no highway—although
> for a brief moment
> on a single August night
> the stars may look down

She lays out the cards on the rough brown table
and tells me to shuffle again. She won't accept
the way they fall. Shuffle again, shuffle well.
She lays out the cards on the rough brown table
in the room with the olive green couch
and the black plastic covered armchair.

> when a child is dying
> the earth gives way
> the laws of physics suspend
> there is no gravity
> that force which holds
> us to the earth no longer exists
> a motel room in an unknown town
> provides no safety only anonymity
> as if this world connects with nothing

The cards with their ancient pictures tell her something that disturbs her.
She doesn't know what, patterns of uncertainty, unease, instability.
"Do you understand this?" she asks. Gravity hangs briefly
in the balance, the air before a storm. ❧

PSALM 60

Thou hast cast us out, and scattered us abroad:

I hadn't expected the ovens to be so small,
big enough for only one body at a time.

Just past Dachau's gate, nuns sing.
Each voice rises, dropping along the notes
of the German hymn, one voice becoming light,

first person singular becoming plural. ℰ

PSALM 61

Hear my crying, O God: give ear unto my prayer.

The look he gives from behind the supermarket counter
is stricken, as if as he rings up my lettuce, scallions, chicken breast,
he thinks I am ringing up his absences and his late papers.
What I notice is how tired he looks, "Been sick?" I ask,
he nods, "and yesterday I worked all day in the freezer,
that didn't help." He asks if I'll be in my office tomorrow
and if he can bring his overdue paper by.
"Of course," I tell him.
I sign my slip, take my groceries, and think
of the essay Greg sent me about the stars, about Neruda's bellringer
pointing to star after star, the sky filling with planets, stars,
suns, constellations turning in the deep night sky.

Today in class students read aloud from papers where
they defined love, friendship, kindness. Each voice
stood out, even the ones that stumbled, rushed, read so softly
we had to strain to hear. One wrote of love as a force which
could change cultures, which could make the world stop turning.

One student reads of her soul-sister, "sometimes we
even hold hands" she reads, "we talk of everything and nothing,
that cute boy, that new face wash." The connections spread
out across the room, and we listen envious as she reads
of being listened to, loved, heard, held.

INTRICACIES OF GRACE

What I want is to reach across the counter,
touch his arm, tell him he works too hard,
tell him that when he isn't in class the chair between
Hannah and Michael is empty, that I miss the way
he turns his head, the way he offers thoughts slowly,
carefully weighing words the way he weighs
scallions, radishes and the heavy iceberg lettuce. &

BEASTS IN SNOW

PSALM 87

Her foundations are upon the holy hills: the Lord loveth the
gates of Sion more than the dwellings of Jacob.

At the art show I fall into a pastel landscape
where the waist-high grey-green sage rises
above the valley, perhaps ancient river bed,
a waiting bottom land.

How often the land appears to hold its breath
in the moment before snow, or the sense of inhalation
on late summer afternoons.

Further down the wall, a model
caught in charcoal, lies on her side
turned away from the viewers,
the curves of shoulder, hip become
a horizon on white paper,
light and shadow. The hollows
at the base of her spine, at the nub
of the anklebone, fill
with darkness, caves on a marble wall.

This landscape excludes me, the sound
of small brittle wings does not rattle
in this air. She lies remote. ✥

PSALM 117

O Praise the Lord, all ye heathen: praise him all ye nations.

There are more this year: tiger swallow tails light
on lilacs, blue iris, columbine, white petunias,
dance in pairs above the driveway, spiral over the garage.

One summer praying mantises stalked our playhouse
tough, bright green hunters with ruthless jaws:
they are good, our mother told us, they eat flies.

We kept an egg case in a jar over the winter
watched it break open and release hundreds
of miniatures, their thread-thin legs and wings knotted together.

One quarter in college, I drew nothing but insects
on zinc etching plates, scratching thin lines through
wax, inking, printing, posting repetitions on the walls,

mosquitoes, black crickets, house flies crept off the press
hung, their heavy paper drying, among
more conventional portraits and landscapes.

BEASTS IN SNOW

The summer I was eight, we stopped play
to watch a just-hatched luna moth on a tall stalk
of grass at the edge of the Jager's lawn.

Its wings unfolded like crumpled paper opening,
its furry antennae felt the foreign air.
Caterpillars, they tell me, dissolve

inside the chrysalis, their bodies becoming
undifferentiated mush until they slowly
re-configure into something new.

I ran home, made my mother leave her ironing,
come back across the road to see
the moth still drying its pale jade wings. ❧

PSALM 127

Except the Lord build the house: their labour is but lost that built it.

At first it could be Atlantis rising,
pushing out of the green undergrowth,
lifting trees on its gray back,
a whale surfacing, white foam falling away,
but we know better, recognize that these ruins
sink slowly down, that these concrete edges erode.

Trees grow now within these foundations
and we can sit on low walls which once
supported doorways, windows, joists, roofs.
We walk on sidewalks which end abruptly nowhere.

Jill sends me photographs of these remains,
says she keeps returning to listen, to see
what might be lost, what she might find.
These pictures come to me wrinkled after weeks
lost in the mail, repackaged in a padded envelope
in Jersey City by some anonymous clerk,
artifacts of artifacts, the way memory
rises and sinks beneath the weight of dailiness.

BEASTS IN SNOW

I remember canoeing on Flagstaff Lake in Maine
where pieces of highway rise up onto the shore,
and descend again, going to farms
long covered by rising water.

In Acme, Wyoming, the four-room school crumbles,
a wall with blackboards stands among rubbled brick.
A metal frame in the yard has no swings.
None of the small company houses remains
along the dirt road lined with tall cottonwood trees.
Rusted cables span the shallow Tongue River—
a suspension bridge men once crossed
to work underground coal mines.

Today half a robin's egg lay in the street
as I walked past, blue against asphalt,
fragile, easily crushed and
gone before I returned. ❧

PSALM 130

Out of the deep have I called to thee, O Lord: Lord, hear my voice.

We find the stumps off the dirt track,
five miles back Tipperary Road,
wood grain crystallized, caught in the soft
afternoon light, growth rings marked in colored rock,
show the wet times and drier ones, though
now, with 15 inches of moisture a year,
this landscape's foreign.

We look out at the hills marked with brick red scoria,
burned rock from some ancient underground fire,
where coal beds spontaneously ignited, and see
near our feet, at the edge of the trail
a low white sego lily; nothing else in bloom.

Too often I have neglected to stop at highway cuts
to look for fossils, sharks teeth from the inland sea,
shells whorling in crumbling sedimentary rock,
small bones impressed into what once was mud.

BEASTS IN SNOW

Too often I have turned instead toward
the new foal rolling in a greening field,
and yesterday I watched Dainis's baby goat,
three days old, springing straight up on legs
too long for her small sleek body. He showed me
currant bushes heavy with green fruit, yellow and purple
iris, blooming pea vines, and the long cabinet
with five drawers cut from the same board
so the grain continues across them all.

What I am trying to tell you is how small this world can be,
and how far past our imaginings. What do I know of trees reaching
200 feet into air thick with moisture, warm even in December, trees
alive in a time before there was December, but only an unnoticed
turning of the earth, an uncounted turning of days, and years? ❧

PSALM 133

Behold, how good and joyful a thing it is: brethen, to dwell in unity!

The Greeks knew the attraction of smooth amber
the way wool rubbed against the golden stone
will spark and snap. Tonight sky's dark umber
clouds roil above the mountains' Prussian bone.
They rise sharp from flat land below, flood-lit
with acid pre-storm light which cuts across
mown fields, tall round bales, the river's silver thread.
In my fingers, amber worry beads count loss
and gain while lightning snaps across the lead
of evening's sky. Sap from ancient trees
oozed out in summer's sun, hardened, dropped
to earth, discovered, smoothed. Attraction weaves
like currents through this solid golden stone
the way the thunder tells us we are not alone. &

Psalm 137

By the waters of Babylon, we sat down and wept: when we remember thee, O Sion.

Nicky writes from Jerusalem that she has missed
being killed by minutes when the bus stop
she had just left was blown up.
She says the university stands heavy, concrete,
safe, just beyond this street.

When I was eleven, a grain elevator exploded in Philadelphia.
My sisters and I looked down into the hole that had once held a basement
while my father explained the mysteries of spontaneous combustion.
I don't know how many died.

I have never been to Jerusalem, never seen sun
on ancient domes and walls, have not bought challah
or Sabbath candles. I have not rattled
Biblical consonants in my mouth as I buy food.
Nicky writes that she will be home soon.

In June in Wyoming, the margins of safety grow.
On the plains all night, you're not likely to freeze to death
or die of thirst. The eastern hills turn green, but as the snow
recedes from the north-facing draws,
whitened bones of winter kill appear,

a deer's rib cage, a skull, tufts of bleaching hair.
In the pellets of a great horned owl, we find
the tiny bones of mice, small birds.
A prickly pear blooms near our feet. ❧

PSALM 141

Lord, I call upon thee: haste thee unto me: and consider my voice
when I cry unto thee.

Let X equal the number of beats in a measure.
See how the beats fit within the bar, mark where each one falls.
Knowing, he says,
removes the mystery.

A singer stands, counts, breathes,
pronounces vowels,
learns all the controllable variables.

One beat per measure creates an underlying pulse.

Let X equal the number of beats,
Y equal pitch, or the way sound
rides on nothing but air.

She holds the F sharp on endless breath,
moves on within the logical measure,
the variables held constant,
until, all small unknowns removed,
only the Unknown remains. &

WHERE WE
& ARE NOW

ASHLAND, PENNSYLVANIA: JANUARY 1966

Why do I need to remember this now,
why go back to that Pennsylvania coal town
where the snow piled in dirty heaps along .
the streets? The sidewalks, cracked brick as I recall
but more than that there's the dark motel with
plywood panels and cramps washing

through me that night while he washed
his hands, held my hand, in ways that now
seem so remote? What was I doing with
an unformed child, here in a dingy town
where no one could reach the doctor with a call?
He only answered letters and told you to bring along

the money. The boy came along
with me and I have to say, washed
my face gently when I threw up, called
out to him, was dazed from too much anesthesia. Now
I could still find that slumping town
in my sleep, and it comes with

sudden and disturbing dreams. An assistant breathed with
difficulty, asthmatically told me to come along
with him down the dark and narrow hall, past towns-
people come for cures for colds, washed
his hands and took away my dress. "Now
breathe," he said, "count backwards, don't call

BEASTS IN SNOW

out a name." Why do I still recall
the stupid signs hung on the ceiling with
cliché sayings that I now
forget? I followed the drugs along
my breath, heard the doctor as he washed
his hands, drifted into unknown towns.

Afterwards the streets wore silence, the town
disappeared behind us. I wanted to recall
the way the falling snow made tears wash
down my face, the way I'd never travel with
this child. But I carry his presence along,
he's with me now.

Dirty snow falls now in this Pennsylvania town.
Along the way, I recall silent snow
falling. A painting: Winter Wash with Child. ❧

BLUE FLAGS

We can not measure coastlines
because the smaller the unit of measurement
the longer the coastline becomes.
Each wash of tide changes how the sand lies,
how the curve at the base of the cliff turns,
how much of that half-buried rock shows.
Come back tomorrow, it will not be the same
unless we measure with the crudest straight lines
and ignore intricacy.

A writer tells me to look at synonyms,
so that we no longer just have blue
but azure, periwinkle, sky, cerulean, Prussian,
navy, baby, cornflower, forget-me-not,
each one stretching the definition into
variations that straight lines just can't follow.
What about turquoise or dark teal? See
how it becomes immeasurable?

I plant the iris bulbs you've given me,
think about how they may bloom next spring.
Blue, you tell me, and I can't decide if
that means the dark ones or the light ones.
My mind traces the ruffled edge of petals,
irregular as a fragile coastline,
the way the saxophone riffs and cries
in that dark bar in Fort Collins
when the young blond musician

tells me how it was to be carried on the music
of the blues piano player, how it was no longer
single notes but synonyms expanding on the smoky air,
how he didn't get tired until just outside of Laramie,
the road unwinding before him like another riff.

Blue flags they're called sometimes, these flowers,
whose petals in sets of three reaching up
curving like small lanterns and three curving
down like small tongues, become a stable six,
a move from odd to even, a change in tempo,
three to six, a little catch
of breath after each three.
Tonight I water them in the cooling August air
and wonder how they'll grow here in the bed
with the mint, the chrysanthemums,
the white and painted daisies.
I watch the soil move and wash,
turn to mud beneath spray.

We can not measure coastlines
or the surprise of iris, the way we find
them wild beside a certain stream
or near old farmsteads where the buildings
are long since gone, the wild ones finer,
more delicate than the ones you've given me,
yet another variation, and always
blue against the blue of sky. ❧

BEASTS IN SNOW

Old Japanese prints show them:
horses standing, heads down
eyes half-closed, small drifts
settling on backs, along long manes.

These horses do not need human
words for "snow," "wind," or "cold"
nor do they care about the way
we wonder at their dark, still bodies
silently waiting out the storm. ❧

JANUARY SONNET

What I love is the complexity of things:
the way the full moon tangles in the winter trees,
or frost forms feathers on the ice-cold glass;
the heron rising from the pond on wings
that seem almost prehistoric, the way bees
swarm and breed, or ants walk among the grass.
Winter's air turns tall trees' branches bright
with ice, as horses stand stoic in the snow.

I love the way a student's look will shift
and stray, come back and concentrate,
the way ideas will crystallize, collect, like light
through prisms, the way a seed will blow
across a pond, settle and then drift
on another breeze before it begins to germinate. ❧

DEFINITIONS OF LOVE

For Brent

"Any fool knows love cannot be defined in ten words
in a dumb textbook," you tell me as you pace
through my kitchen one day after school.
Your notebooks spill across my table
as the late winter sun sets behind the mountains,
still covered with new snow,
and I remember my son's phone call last week
from hundreds of miles away when he told me
that if two people in different places drop plumb lines
which extend long enough, these lines will meet
at the center of the earth.

Long ago in a college dance class, the teacher used to tell us,
"feel the plumb line from the ceiling through
your body to the floor." We moved up and down
that line, aware always of its stretched presence,
our pliés and relevés lifted up, up
until our bodies came close to levitation.

You pace my kitchen, your long-boned body
ranging in and out of light and shadow.
I hear in your voice your longing to be out,
up in the mountains, following a trail
to a lake, a peak, a summer snow field.
Lost Twin Lakes sit beneath high rock walls
and early in the morning the trout rise, leaving
circles, widening rings as the fish submerge.
We've camped here at this lake just at tree line
and watched dislodged rock clatter
down those deep gray granite walls.

BEASTS IN SNOW

When I learned to ski the teacher said,
"Follow the fall line down the slope, the way
a snow ball would. Keep the line there in your mind
as you move across it," the way our dancers' bodies
turned and bent across that fine invisible cord.

Those plumb lines dropped through the earth
could miss, just might miss if the earth were not
what it is. We might not connect, touch the rock
or feel within us the widening circles of the morning's rise.
But that is how it is: It is no ten-word definition
which draws you up that trail to where
you spend the night looking at the summer stars,
blurred to cotton balls after you have taken off your glasses.
There in the August sky each point connects with
imaginary lines until you, lying there
on the rocky ground, are lulled to sleep
like just another star. ❧

CROSS-COUNTRY SKIING AT ANTELOPE BUTTE

Today I saw trees weathered gray
and yellow the way ponderosa pines
color when they die. They turn
and twist along the grain or with
prevailing wind and eventually the gold
wears down to only gray or, if the light

is right, to silver. Today the light
touched each branch, the slim gray
trunks of aspen and sharp gold
streaks in dead branches, old stumps of pine.
I followed the trail among them with
new snowshoe tracks ahead, but at the turn

I went east into thicker woods. No marked turn,
I broke trail through fine light
snow, skis hidden and emerging
with the slightest swish, only gray
branches heavy with needles, ponderosa pine
between me and air. The sun soft gold

in southern sky, only barely gold
in deep mid-winter zero air and it would turn
colder still. It's a wonder that the pines
stay green, that mid-winter's meager light's
enough to keep them all from turning gray.
I skied along this narrow path with

BEASTS IN SNOW

only weeks-old tracks to help me with
direction. Ahead a splash of gold,
a fallen trunk, its outer layers gone gray.
Newly dead this year, it will turn
and fade, rot slowly in this deep dry light
beneath these living pines.

Ahead the trail escaped the pines
and another set of ski tracks joined with
mine. An open meadow full of light,
the sun gone white, no longer gold
and colder now. The wind turned
sharp, the sky to gray.

Ski trails among gray pines
turn sharp with wind
and winter's pale gold light. ☙

IF THE LION COULD SPEAK

"If the lion could speak we would not understand him."
                                        Wittgenstein

Your thick back rises above me.
I see how your muscles join the bone,
how the hair grows in that one triangular patch,
see the scar below the right scapula
where you scraped it thirty years ago
on a rock while you swam naked
in the warm amber water of Lake Nineveh,
just before, treading water, we coupled like slick young seals.

Your eyes, above your gray beard, watch
the horizon, follow the line of plains,
see the great black swathes left by the summer's grass fires,
entire hills north of Hardin and the place where
the fire crossed all eight lanes of highway.
You raise your head to the smoking air,
thinking of the fires still burning in the mountains.

I run my fingers across your scarred back,
wake at night and think the house is burning.
Ash lies on window sills and tables.
You sleep beside me in the heavy air.
Smoke rises white against the dark night sky.
The stars obscured; there is no moon. ✑

SUNSETS IN A SUMMER OF FOREST FIRES

Each evening reminds us that trees are burning
somewhere to the west of us. During the day, the air
chokes us, smells so heavily of smoke
we turn to check the kitchen, furnace, candles.

Clouds loft and tear in slanting light
turn red, cerise, salmon, coral, later dropping
into purple, charcoal, navy, while above
them, the evening star burns sharp and white.

I can't really tell you how it is to wake
and think the house is burning, but
like the man who dreams his dead wife has returned
to share his bed and wakes to find her gone

we resist belief, rush to find a hidden
fire, the forgotten smoldering sauce pan
but in the end, it's only ash from trees
becoming tomorrow's blood-red sky. ❧

PLANTING

for Stephanie

The moon is full tonight
and catches in the branches
of the Chinese Elms in my backyard.
I look out my kitchen window
and watch its white light rise.

Wyoming, February, the air's still
cold, new snow blows
across the sidewalk and our frozen footprints
from yesterday's thaw prove
that we have left the house.

"I should," she said, " be writing
instead of getting gardening books
from the library." But, I want to say,
what better way to prepare
the soil for spring?

Think of new asparagus,
heavy-headed dahlias, cosmos,
the rich colors of zinnias,
tall stems of snapdragons,
or bean vines curling along a string.

Writing this comes as easily
as a rising winter moon, a blue
shadow on snow, or the way
new lettuce unfurls its small green hands
upward toward a cloudless summer sky. ❧

RITUALS

for Nora Mitchell

Emily told me once that if you do something twice
it becomes a ritual. She, Nora and I laughed over Thai food,
tofu and hot pepper, shrimp curry the way
we have twice now when I have flown into Burlington
to sleep at their house, talk to their cats, walk with Bear the dog.
In February we walked along the shore of Lake Champlain
and remembered September's sailboats, spinnakers billowing
blowing, filling with wind. Then we're home
to dinner—chopsticks optional.

All three of us teachers, we listened to Emily's student
read the poem about the first time her blind daughter went skiing,
the mother's fear fills the room, her concentration on the physical,
the snap of buckles, zipping of coats, the click of ski bindings,
each sound palpable, real, there.

So now in June, I sit at an early morning picnic table,
watch the sun refract through ponderosa pines, splinter
and reconnect. Can a sunrise be a ritual?
Can acknowledging a sunrise?
Birds whose names I do not know celebrate the returning light.
Daniel and Jim and I sat in the lodge kitchen last night
reading new poems as if it had not been a year, as if we'd never left,
as if, like the returning sun, this forms daily ritual.

But this is about more than Thai food, sisters.
It's about how we connect across poems,
Nora's hand on my arm, "I love," she says,
"the way your mind works" and suddenly I am stripped
as if she has taken off my clothes.
I watched Daniel read to me last night, his voice shy, daring,
allowing me in.

So attend to this: stir your coffee carefully
watch the spoon pull subtle oils across the surface,
taste it, hold the spoon to someone's lips.
Watch the way her mouth curls around the bowl,
take it in, hold your hand to her mouth and feel
skin on skin, the arc of teeth against the line of your hand.
But I think this has little to do with whose mouth this is,
whose hand, whose bone (how much does the skeleton of the
hand change from person to person?) So what I mean is this:
it could be Emily's mouth or Daniel's.
Think of the words that people speak.
Think of what it means to touch.
Daniel sits on the floor by Jennifer, his hand on her leg,
her painted toes curling against his fingers.

BEASTS IN SNOW

Pay attention, because we do not know the texts we read.
The skin of my breasts pulls tight in the sun
pulls tight against the revelation of these words.
It may be no more than knowing I can spend my nights
curled against another body, the small hairs on his
lower back warm along my belly.
It may be no more than feeling my son's new
whiskers beneath my fingers.
Baby fingers once sought my face, needed
to be in my mouth as this child nursed
and suckled at my breast,
another necessary ritual.

Today I shocked the children by taking off my shirt,
letting the sun form itself to shoulder, scapula and backbone.
I am too old to worry about convention now, too old
to deny my flesh the caress of air and wind,

just as a few hours ago, on Lake Champlain,
the evening wind caught bright spinnakers,
filled them with air, and moved on. &

SWEET BELL PEPPERS
for Daniel

Today the falling leaves seduce me into thinking
that they are more beautiful than they have ever been,
that the soft apricot of the mountain ash and its
bright berries are new this year. But this autumnal
beauty has as much to do with words as leaves and air,
grey sky preparing for rain, as much to do with
you sitting at my kitchen table asking if you will
still be calling to read me poems when you are old.

When you are old, you mean when you are thirty or
thirty-five, an eternity from sixteen and all I can do is look at you
and answer, "I hope so." What you don't know is that
I've watched you sitting at my computer, thinking,
your hands in your long, too long, straight hair.
Or I have listened as you mumbled to yourself
while I diced chicken in the kitchen.
I broke open the red bell pepper,
its shell opening flower-like around
the hive of seeds, "Look, "I said, taking it to you,
"look, it is so beautiful."

It startled you, I think, to hear me
ask you if you had ever held cut kiwi
up to the window, let the light filter
through green flesh, a small, circular piece of sea water.

Years before you were born, I wrote letters on pink tissue paper
typing on a portable Smith-Corona, keys so hard to press
the whole room shook, that boy in Chicago, older than I
but still a boy, treasuring them all. Later, there are all
those drawings, even then I was in love
with rounded flesh, curves, repeating seeds.
I drew them again, again filling sketch books,
caressing the paper with pencil, pen and charcoal.

And so tonight I slice them, red and green together
and listen to you type, see you smile at me as you
finish your history paper, the one due tomorrow,
and remember that my friend in Brooklyn writes,
"Isn't teaching all about love?"
Listen now, the wind's picked up;
yellow leaves rain outside my door,
bright lights against the greying sky. ❧

STONE DREAMS
with the Central Middle School Sixth Grade

Today I asked the children to tell me
stone dreams. "Look," I said, "at the stone I have placed on your
desk. Does it dream about the streaks of color,
the veins of green or red along its sides, does it dream of
the boulder it once was?
What would you dream if you were this stone?"

I read them a poem by another teacher who asks the same question
and whose students tell him " stones don't dream."

I draw circles on the board. "See," I say, "the way
he remembers stones and students,
remembers childhood chestnuts gathered like shiny stones,
filling the bag until it breaks
and he sits on the ground holding the
burnished solid spheres
and remembers again?"

The thin blond girl writes,
"My dreams are like stones, strong, and round,
I treasure them, like stones in colored boxes."
Another child writes "I am a little person, I walk into
rooms filled with crystal chips inside the stone."

BEASTS IN SNOW

and then the small tense boy with glasses writes
five lines, tears the notebook paper small,
small enough to fit the little poem
about a stone underground, in the dark, under
the earth, ground pressing down
then suddenly the stone is
"dreaming of a flower."

The room stills,
dark smell of loam and earth falls
at our feet while brilliant dahlias bloom, and imagined
color flares against the dreaming stone,
orange lilies and Christmas amaryllis.
"What do you think?" I ask the class
"I think" Stephanie says, "it's about
sometimes we think we know a person
and we really don't." &

TEACHING READING

Ginger root gnarls in my hand
above the cilantro, parsley, eggplant
dark as midnight
dust clings to my fingers.
Change slips and jingles in the check-out line.

Ellen hated herself so much that when
I, as her teacher, asked her to do math,
she bit her hand and retreated
to the nest of blankets in the corner.
Curling her bird-bone legs and arms
up tight against her, we might forget
that she was there.

One day she asked to learn to read,
eleven years old, but time meant nothing.
In rivers some water continues swirling, caught
in a backwash, an eddy, a violent pool
behind a rock.
"Teach me to read," she asked.

I slice onion, sauté, stir,
add ginger, garlic,
the kitchen fills with smells
red and green peppers, chicken.

Ellen's thin neck curves above her desk.
She learns the story of the princess she wants to be.
She will not take the pages home but asks
me to keep them for her in my teacher's desk.

There is no happy ending here.

Day by day she works,
builds sentences with word cards,
long white lines across the classroom floor.
She learns not to bite herself.
Her mother dies.

I boil rice and set the table.

Once day at recess in the small schoolyard,
she stayed close to my side, repeating,
"Hold my hand, Jane, hold my hand, please,
so I don't get lost," as if the smallest
human touch could save her.

I have created an imaginary meal.
What nourishment does writing bring?

In the face of bravery, we must fall back,
decode those marks on paper.
Once again, she steps out across the ice.

On the last day of school, late June,
the Philadelphia magnolias gone, the air humid,
thick, the buses wait. She turns, stops,
"See you tomorrow, Jane," she says,
"See you tomorrow."
She climbs on finally and is gone. ✑

ROSES AND TULIPS
For Melinda

It is all so ordinary:
the men installing the new furnace,
the broken spring on the storm door,
(they must hold it open while they struggle
the bulky box strapped to the dolly over the threshold).
One of them comes into the living room
to tell us that the water will be off for an hour.

The air begins to chill
and you pull your coat over your knees
as we discuss Faulkner—
your English paper,
Emily's decaying life, and
a desiccated, long-dead rose.
This is a paper I have assigned, read, re-read,
written a hundred times, and yet,
today I am not the teacher
and I listen as you struggle,
annotate, underline, re-word,
until finally, you begin to tell me
that you are divorcing,
that you have no money,
that your red-haired son flies
comet-like across your day,
freed now from his father's harping on his faults,
that your daughter came in last night
and talked and talked in ways she never had before.

BEASTS IN SNOW

"I just want to be his friend, Mama," she says,
more afraid of hurting than of being hurt.
You wish you could tell her friendship is possible
and think maybe it is for her.

The house grows colder.
I begin to wish I'd put on a sweater,
the tip of my nose begins to chill
even on this mild February day.
The tulips you have brought me
flame on the end table
as you tell me how little you have to spend for food.
What is Faulkner in the face of courage?

On the phone you said you had so much to say
but you didn't have the tools,
the ways of putting grief on paper.

Now I lend you a book on how to write,
how to translate thought to words,
as if with words we can each define our lives,
tell stories of elusive pasts,
let words, like tulips, flame against decay.

And I think of that man from Mississippi,
writing of death, of dreams
and finally, what in our ordinary lives,
we might call love.

For Daniel, Again

"You shouldn't do this if you don't love to cut onions."
Quote from a cooking teacher

Feel the sharp bite of the black pen across rough white paper.
Watch the way ink smudges, spreads, swirls into letters
of the alphabet, connecting into words, into sounds we hear
in that dark place behind our eyes, as if our hands are fettered
to the nerves along the arm, across the shoulders, and through the skull.

Taste the way the spring day rises from the page, dogwood,
slippery elm, dogtooth violet, lilac, mud, manure, dull
thud of a door closing down the road, the strong good
smell of coffee, the heft of light across a table set
with blue plates, a bowl of oranges, pale green apples, white
cups, a vase of daisies. Do not forget

that this is imaginary: if you don't love the light
smell of onions on soft clean hands, the way the dicings fall
like sharp white teeth, don't pick up the pen, don't linger
over words, or let caught thought rest between your fingers. ❧

CONVERGENCE

On the day after September 11, 2001,
passengers on the bus from Phoenix
to Boston heard Yo Yo Ma
practice the new Eliot Carter cello concerto,
his Stradivarius between his knees,
score spread on the seat across the aisle.

Some might have tried to sleep, their senses
dulled by the straight line of interstate,
static geometry beneath the wheels,
but at the same moment a resonance
might have begun beneath a shoulder blade, a muscle,
within a chest, a sound caught and spun,
the way a frequency of light repeats
against our lowered lids.

Beyond the bus windshield, the parallel lanes
of the highway seem to merge,
but never meet, the way
vapor trails of jets streak
unraveling over blue, the way
we might ask for mercy from
some unknown god, offering up
these soft white trails as smoke from sacrifice.

I touch my son's strong shoulder, and
smell coffee rising in the kitchen air,
feel the wind of coming winter on my face.

This is not the life of an Afghani woman
who can not find enough to eat.
Her life does not intersect mine, she can not,
does not desire connection. Convergence will
not occur—the geometry of politics.

Smoke from fires in New York, Kabul, Kandahar,
in Washington, in Bethlehem, in Hebron, rise,
rise, continue rising in the autumn sky,
the way that line of melody continues
beyond that moving bus. ॐ

THE AMBIVALENCE OF BEAUTY
October 7, 2001

On the day the bombs began,
I broke eggs for breakfast,
dropped their contents
into a plastic bowl,
and held the broken halves
of shells in my cupped hands,
brown, white, palest green,
fresh from Trudy's chickens,
light as petals, as snow falling.

Falling, the way the halves
of robins' eggs fall, each spring
from the spruce tree
before I even know the adults
have built their nests,
tiny turquoise shells
so light they blow into the street,
where, if we don't stop
to pick them up, they're crushed
by unsuspecting feet or turning wheels.

I hold the green one to the window
see its fine translucence and
remember once seeing,
in the bright beam of a pen light,
the tiny heart
of an unhatched parrot beating. ❧

ATHEISM

I worship gravity, sunlight and love.
Consider how my own body rests on earth,
how a flower turns toward sun above
the clouds, opening in a measured birth
of color, petunias, dahlias, morning glory.
Consider how our children stay within our reach,
how we find our babies' hands, how we see
the predictable growth of trees, each
one lifting from its solid roots held tight
in the dark loam's grasp. Consider the way water flows
downhill, joining rivulet, stream, wild bright
torrent, ocean. It's how the sweet pea grows
or fish among deep coral, or stars at night.
Forces far beyond my tiny grasp and
yet, because of these, I hold your human hand. ❧

WHAT WE ARE GIVEN
for R.

We are confounded by the mysteries of memory:

A monk descending Mt. Fujiyama at dawn
becomes, in a different time and place,
the way we leave each other without warning.

You feel the slanting morning light across your face,
jam cold hands into your jacket pockets.
   He smiles, bows, turns and walks silently away.

Some things remain:
   The way I have felt each knuckle of your long-boned hand,
   or the way water once cradled us in that woodland pond.

We can not give back what we are given,
and so, in this windowless classroom, where
my students bend over their mid-term tests, I feel
Mt. Fuji's wind across my face and see,
with your eyes, the small saffron-robed monk descend. ℰ

JANE ELKINGTON WOHL lives in Sheridan, Wyoming, with her pediatrician husband, Barry. She teaches English at Sheridan College and teaches poetry and fiction in the Goddard College M.F.A. in Writing program, Plainfield, Vermont. Her writing has been published in numerous small journals and anthologies; including *Leaning into the Wind*, *Woven on the Wind*, *The Women's Review of Books*, *Teachers and Writers*, *Owen Wister Review*, *The Lyric*, *Green Fuse*, and *Tap-Joe*.

This book was simultaneously printed in two editions.

A special limited edition of only 200 copies was bound in Largo Teal kidskin Kivar 7 and embossed with crown silver foil. Each copy was individually signed by the author and hand-numbered.

A jacketed softcover trade edition was issued simultaneously. It is bound in ten-point stock and wrapped in a four-color dust jacket, coated with a matte finish.

The text is eleven-point Berkeley Oldstyle Book by the International Type Company. Display type is Adobe Trajan and Missale AS Incana. The book is printed on seventy-pound New Life Opaque, a recycled, acid-free paper, by Central Plains Book Manufacturing.